News Crew

Teaching Tips

Orange Level 6

This book focuses on the phonemes **/u_e/ue/ew/**.

Before Reading

- Discuss the title. Ask readers what they think the book will be about. Have them briefly explain why.
- Ask readers to sort the words on page 3. Read the sounds and words together.

Read the Book

- Encourage readers to break down unfamiliar words into units of sound. Then, ask them to string the sounds together to create the words.
- Urge readers to point out when the focused phonics phonemes appear in the text.

After Reading

- Encourage children to reread the book independently or with a friend.
- Ask readers to name other words with /u_e/, /ue/, or /ew/ phonemes. On a separate sheet of paper, have them write the words out.

© 2024 Booklife Publishing
This edition is published by arrangement with Booklife Publishing.

North American adaptations © 2024 Jump!
5357 Penn Avenue South
Minneapolis, MN 55419
www.jumplibrary.com

Decodables by Jump! are published by Jump! Library.
All rights reserved. No part of this book may be reproduced
in any form without written permission from the publisher.

Library of Congress Cataloging-in-Publication Data
is available at www.loc.gov or upon request from
the publisher.

ISBN: 979-8-88996-864-1 (hardcover)
ISBN: 979-8-88996-865-8 (paperback)
ISBN: 979-8-88996-866-5 (ebook)

Photo Credits
Images are courtesy of Shutterstock.com. With thanks to Getty Images, Thinkstock Photo and iStockphoto. Cover – Aggapom Poomitud, 4x6. 4–5 – gorodenkoff. 6–7 – withGod, Krakenimages.com. 8–9 – gorodenkoff, simonkr. 10–11 – jan kranendonk, Billion Photos. 12–13 – SpeedKingz, REALDEE. 14–15 – Omeer, Travelpixs. 16 – Shutterstock.

Can you sort all the words on this page into two groups?

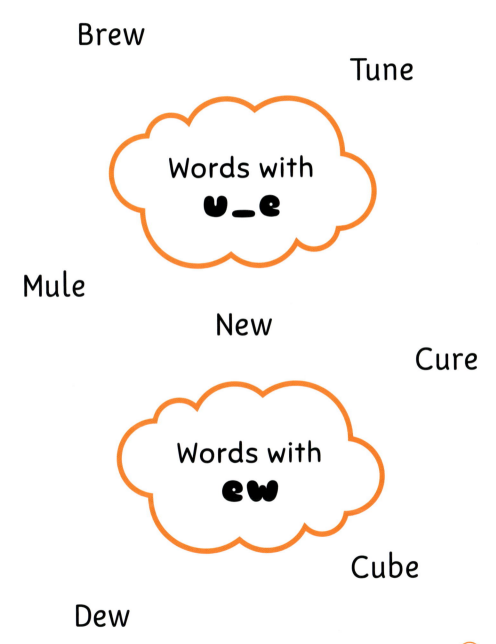

Brew

Tune

Mule

New

Cure

Cube

Dew

Do you ever think about the people who tell us the news? They have an important job. They help us understand what is happening around us.

There are a few different jobs on a news crew. There are lots of people who we do not see on the TV screen.

Some people tell us the news. They explain true things that have happened to us. When they are on air, they must not panic.

They might read a teleprompter. It has cues on it so they do not forget what to say. They must speak clearly.

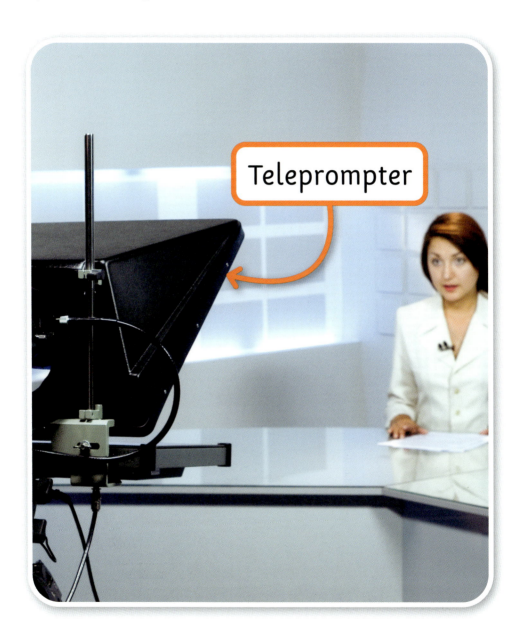

Some people tell us when it is going to rain or be hot. They can tell us if a storm is near.

On the TV, we see them pointing at a map. However, they have to point at a green screen without looking.

Some people have the job of getting it all on film. They use a lens to film the people we see on TV.

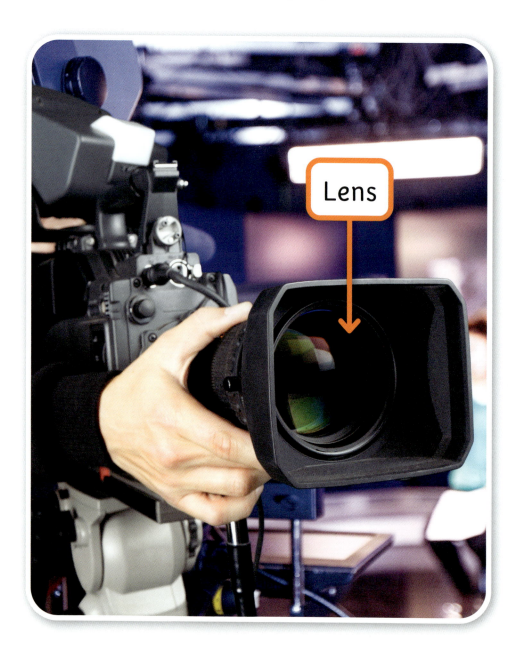

They might film in the newsroom. They might go out to film an event at a new spot each day.

There are people on the news crew who help come up with what to say on air. They make sure the crew tells us things that are true.

Some people tell the crew what to do. They choose which parts of the film to use and which parts to exclude.

Exclude means to leave out.

Staying on top of the most current news can be a big job. To do it well, the crew has to act as a team.

All the people on a news crew have value. Without them, we might never hear what is happening around the planet. Thank you, news crew!

Can you name the missing letters for each word?

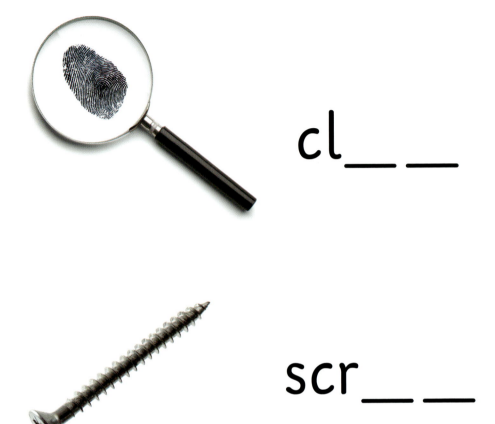

cl___ ___

scr___ ___

c___b___